Science

What Are Atoms?

By Lisa Trumbauer

Consultant
Linda Bullock
Science Curriculum Specialist

New York • • Sydney
Mexico • Hong Kong
Danbury, Connecticut

Designer: Herman Adler Design
Photo Researcher: Caroline Anderson
The photo on the cover shows a flower made of atoms.

Library of Congress Cataloging-in-Publication Data

Trumbauer, Lisa, 1963-
   What are atoms? / by Lisa Trumbauer ; consultant, Linda Bullock.
     p. cm. — (Rookie read-about science)
   Includes index.
   ISBN 0-516-23617-2 (lib. bdg.)   0-516-24665-8 (pbk.)
   1. Atoms—Juvenile literature. 2. Matter—Constitution—Juvenile
literature. I. Title. II. Series.
   QC173.16.T78 2004
   539.7—dc22
                          2004001217

CHILDREN'S PRESS, and ROOKIE READ-ABOUT®,
and associated logos are trademarks and or registered trademarks
of Scholastic Library Publishing. SCHOLASTIC and associated logos
are trademarks and or registered trademarks of Scholastic Inc.

1 2 3 4 5 6 7 8 9 10 R 13 12 11 10 09 08 07 06 05 04

What is the smallest thing
you can imagine? An ant?

Smaller!

A grain of salt?

Keep going!

Atoms are the smallest things on Earth.

You can't see them, even under a microscope.

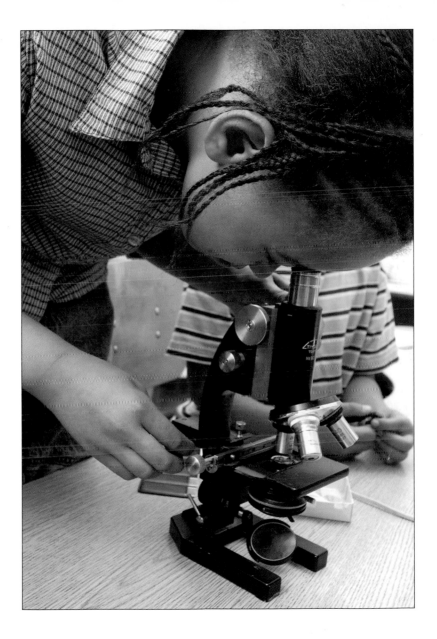

Atoms are the building blocks that make all matter on Earth. Matter is what things are made of.

Everything is made of matter. You are, too!

A jungle gym is made of matter.

neutrons   nucleus   protons   electrons

Parts of an atom

Every atom has three parts. These parts are protons, neutrons (NOO-trahns), and electrons (ee-LECK-trahns).

Protons and neutrons are in the nucleus (NOO-klee-us). The nucleus is the center of an atom. Electrons move around the nucleus.

Not all atoms are the same. They have different numbers of protons, neutrons, and electrons.

Buildings are made of atoms.

Food is made of atoms.

Different kinds of atoms
make different things.

Atoms join together
to make molecules (MOL-
uh-kyools). Molecules
made of one kind of
atom are called elements.

This lamppost has an element
in it. It is called iron.

Copper is an element.
A penny is made of copper.

Helium is an element, too.
Some balloons are filled
with helium.

Hydrogen is an element.
Oxygen is an element.

These two elements join
together to make water.

A waterfall in Yosemite National Park

Remember, molecules are made of atoms.

A molecule of water is made of two hydrogen atoms and one oxygen atom.

There are billions of
molecules in a drop of water.

The air you blow into a balloon is a gas.

Some molecules make things that are solid.

Other molecules make liquids or gases.

Rocks are a solid.

Molecules in a solid are
packed close together. They
hardly move. This helps a
solid keep its shape.

Molecules in a liquid are close together, too. But they can move. That is why a liquid changes its shape.

Orange juice is a liquid.

Some molecules don't stay close together at all. They move around freely.

These molecules make gases like the air we breathe.

You can fly a kite when air moves fast.

Atoms make molecules.
Molecules make you.
They make plants, animals,
water, and air, too.

Everything is made of
atoms and molecules.

29

Words You Know

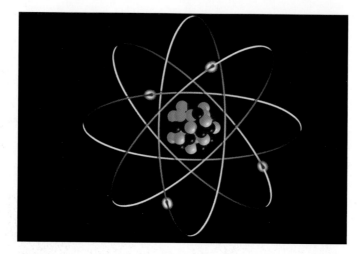

atom

compound

copper

iron

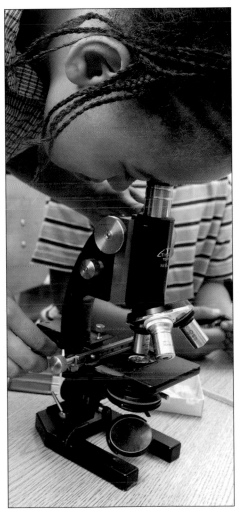

microscope

31

Index

About the Author

Lisa Trumbauer is the author of over 200 books for children, many of which are science-related. Formerly an editor with *Scientific American Library Books*, Lisa went on to edit several science programs for early learners. In addition, she has written science books about animals, plants, the Earth, and the physical sciences. Lisa and her husband, Dave, live in New Jersey with their dog, Blue, and their cats, Cosmo and Cleo.

Photo Credits

Photographs © 2004: Animals Animals/Raymond Mendez: 3; David R. Frazier/Mike Penney: 19, 30 bottom left; Dembinsky Photo Assoc.: 22 (Dan Dempster), 29 (Bill Lea), 12 (Patti McConville); Ellen B. Senisi: cover, 5, 7, 9, 13, 25, 31 right; James Levin/Studio 10: 16, 30 bottom right; Photo Researchers, NY: 10, 30 top (Scott Camazine), 24 (Rod Planck); PhotoEdit: 21 (Robert Brenner), 14, 26, 31 left (Tony Freeman), 17 (Spencer Grant).